7 Pillars

of a

Successful Marriage

© 2010 by Peter and Jane

Published by PMM

Printed by PMM

All rights Reserved. No part of this publication may be reproduced or utilized in any form or by any means electronic or mechanical, including photocopying, recording or by any information storage and retrieval system now known or hereafter invented without expressed permission of the copy right holder.

Unless otherwise stated, scripture quotations are from New International Version.

Cover design by family rebuild team

To get in touch with the authors: wangaruro2000@yahoo.com

Dedicated to

All those who value family stability and who honour the family structure of the family government given by God

For further communication please email; familyrebuild@yahoo.co.uk

Table of contents

Introduction i-v

1 Chapter one- Love 6
Introduction, self-giving love, passion, intimacy, commitment

2 Chapter two- Vision 18
Introduction, Man and the vision, woman in the vision, Common vision.

3 Chapter three - Prayer 23
Introduction, Prayer of faith, consistence, persistence, and unity.

4 Chapter four – Communication 33
Introduction, Bridge analogy, levels of talk, listening, communication methods.

5 Chapter Five - Finances 47
Making money, Financial needs, Accountability

6 Chapter Six – Character 53
Introduction, technology, Tongue and character

7 Chapter Seven – Respect 62

8 Chapter Eight – Reinforcing the Pillars 68

Introduction

Many have cried on the phone and in counselling offices as they wondered whether they made a grave mistake to be married to their spouses. Yet there is always a re-sounding echo saying, "Remember the day you walked down the isle of that cathedral or church and pledged allegiance to each other before God and men and then you side by side walked amidst jubilation". The guilt of failure, negligence, ignorance and arrogance has haunted many couples.

It is not the will of God for you to have Jesus as the master of your life and the devil as the master of your marriage. We have no words to highlight the importance of laying a solid marital foundation before marriage. Greater still is the enrichment marital counselling that continues in marriage life which provides reinforcement against unfruitful relationships.

God is so concerned about how we live in families such that he gave us his word as a manual. He has also given gifts to his servants to equip marriages within the frame work of his word.

The purpose of this book is to give reinforcement pillars for a successful marriage. It is true that any structure needs reinforcement if it has to be firm and fulfil its purpose. Marriage is such an important engagement or institution that it is only out of ignorance that one would ever build it without a strong base support.

The book will act as an appetizer and will leave the reader thirsting for more of the kind. The seven pillars that it reveals are :(Love, Vision, Prayer, Communication, Character, Finances, Respect). We may not claim excellence in our marriage but we have good command of each of the pillar and our daily target is to live true to the same.

We therefore welcome you to read through each of the pillar with a positive mental attitude and readiness to improve your relationship. We invite those who are preparing to marry to read this book during their courtship and they will brightly enter into marriage. We challenge couples whether enjoying marriage or facing challenges to discuss each of the pillars and make relevant practical steps for this may shield their relationship from being in a rut.

Author's Prayer for your marriage.

Father we pray for the marriage of the person reading this book that it shall experience an uplifting. We declare that the challenges addressed in this book shall never defeat this marriage. Our father thank you for the victory given and we ask that this marriage will become an example for others to emulate. Let their children be mighty in the land. In Jesus name we pray.

Reality in marriage

People have largely been shown an awful picture of marriage and left to wonder if there is a successful marriage. Some young people have seen violence at home, others have seen and heard divorces publicized over the media where the permanence of marriage has been discredited. The learned and the unlearned, atheist, religious and their clergy have equally failed to enjoy the sweetness of marriage. This loudly rings a bell, Gong! Gong! Gong!

Doesn't it? There must be something that people are missing in order to enjoy a successful marriage!

Statistics tell us that second marriage is twice as likely to end up in divorce as the first one. People have frequently asked whether somebody can really enjoy a successful marriage. Others have embraced the secular influence in their lives to the extent that they think marriage cannot work. Whatever the preposition that one has marriage was designed to be lived here on earth not in heaven. God made both the male and the female and intended that they enjoy the companionship. It means therefore that if people are not enjoying a successful marriage then there is something amiss in the way they handle their relationship.

> *Marital Love is a project that closes in death.*

Certainly a successful marriage is not one where perfection reigns for we can all consent that there are no perfect people living on the earth. We are all prone to weakness and failure because of our human nature. Nevertheless the peculiarity in God's creation is that man is equipped with enormous ability to network, complement each other and team play until they produce a harmonious relationship. This ability is the tool which produces a successful marriage.

> *None of us has an ideal marriage but the path towards it is open to all.*

Harmonious relationship therefore exists only when people resolve to unselfishly work on it. Let no one be deceived that there are no successful marriages. Remember success in marriage emanates from discipline, hard work and self giving love. There are many couples who are not willing to pay the cost of marriage maintenance and yet desire to enjoy a good relationship. It is not a wish but the purposeful action that produces a thriving relationship. There is something that a couple must do in order to enjoy a successful marriage. I welcome you on board to read, meditate and evaluate your marriage against each of the pillars below with a quest to successfully enjoy your marital relationship.

Peter Wangaruro and Dr. Jane Wangaruro

CHAPTER 1

Pillar One

Love

From an English dictionary love is defined as a deep affection or fondness. Other words that have been used for love are admiration, attachment, friendship, liking, and devotion. These are just but different segments (branches) of love and none of them can stand for all others. Love can also be divided in branches of commitment, intimacy, and romance. It will only be sweet if all segments are functional in a coherent way. Using one segment of love and ignoring the others will produce a malnourished relationship.

A successful marriage could only be possible where all the segments of love are allowed to play. This Pillar of Love is one of the main ingredients in a marriage relationship as it bonds a couple together as friends. In marriage two people seek to operate on a common platform through agreement. It is not easy to agree if people do not like it.

A couple that will move together and have an attachment must have a great liking for it. Friends do like each other and have overly fondness for each other. This pillar therefore calls for spouses to have this fondness and an inseparable devotion to each other. In marriage two people seek to operate on a common platform through agreement. It is not easy to agree if people do not like it. A couple that will move together and have an attachment must have a great liking for it.

Love like a magnet has an attraction effect which creates admiration and deep affection. It not only draws people together but it also supplies the ingredients that hold them together. Any couple that is married and miss the dimension where they admire each other will certainly struggle to remain together. Where there is no attraction in marriage then there is repulsion. I really thank God who has enabled me and Jane to progress. It was difficult when we first started but we deliberately developed this quality which tends to keep our marriage younger. Do not be under any illusion that we have made it or that we live in love paradise. Love is our project until the end for there are times when this switch trips due various overloads.

Marital love is a project that closes in death

Self giving love

A famous quote made by the late US president John F. Kennedy back in the early 1960's states: "Ask not what your country can do for you, but what you can do for your country" I believe that President Kennedy wanted to see the Americans involved and active in building their country which would in *return bring good for them. Genuine love in marriage is that self giving quality that it seeks to give rather than receive from a spouse.* Each spouse needs to put this 'Kennedy question' in marriage context if their marriage is to be successful. Ask not what your marriage; spouse, children, relationship can do for you, but what you can do in each of the area under consideration.

"God demonstrated his love for us in that while we were yet sinners Christ died for us" Romans 5:8.

The scripture above shows that love can be demonstrated through giving or sacrificing one's own for the sake of the other one. Most marriages are rocked at this position where spouses are rigid and fail to quit from the selfishness canoe. A measure of successful marriage is demonstrated when a spouse seeks to make positive contribution in the relationship despite the cost. It may mean forgiving one's spouse, standing in the gap, or helping with house chores without complaining. Love that does not have visible features is empty and does not reinforce the stability of a marriage relationship. This means that a successful marriage is not a theory lesson rather it is like a workshop where theories are applied practically.

> *Love must be demonstrated, felt, received and then enjoyed*

Men have exploited very little elements of love and as a result have missed a balanced loving relationship. This has been because of ignorance or cultural practices and also media influence. For example media portrays love on the aspect of romance while most cultures required men to demonstrate commitment to the institution. I will explain love as jig saw puzzle consisting of three main pieces namely passion, intimacy and commitment. Men will not experience success in their relationship if they dwell on one piece of the puzzle.

1) Passion

Passion is that magnetic sort of attraction that makes a spouse to like being together with the other one. It is a pull that comes from soul connection and based on physical or emotional factors. In some people it may be termed as obsession, excitement or craze that creates a romantic feeling.

Romance is that creation of an atmosphere which thrills one's feelings and emotions. It catches every attention in the soul's department and makes one to feel loved. It is a personal expression of love through sweet talk, a whisper of those heart reaching messages, being full of affection and having an eye catching state. It is an act of demonstrating friendliness. A lasting love relationship needs to cultivate passion beyond honey moon days.

How romantic are you to your spouse?

A woman cherishes to hear her husband express his love to her outside the bedroom walls. It is important for a man to develop love language towards his wife. A loving man should be able to verbally tell his wife that she looks awesome when they have dressed to go somewhere. Men have soft love spots and their feeling quickly and easily respond to the beauty in a woman. Unfortunately in some traditions men are unable to express their feelings and satisfaction due to cultural bondage. A liberated man should go past cultural limitation and male chauvinism that never regarded women as important.

a) Have you written a text message to your spouse today?

b) When did you last send a card to your spouse?

c) How do you demonstrate your love to your spouse?

A Christian woman should strive to have the inner beauty for that is what defines her character but at the same time she should also be concerned with her outward appearance. The outer beauty has a lot of meaning for that is what people see first. The wayward woman as described in the scriptures trades on her outer beauty and she misses any inner beauty a thing that makes her to continue in sexual slavery. Those who come her way fall into a dip pit. Outer beauty without the inner beauty might attract every sensual demon that hinders character formation. The Bible in the book of Proverbs chapter seven warns us against this behaviour as portrayed by the immoral woman.

> *Outer beauty without inner beauty is no beauty at all*

In reality, a successful marriage will have a couple who are not skewed on one side because though we have heaven as our destiny our feet trends on earthly paths until rapture or death. It is therefore important for spouses to be elegant and that does not mean being expensive. The determination to remain attractive to a spouse is a project worth taking in marriage. I urge people to carry the beauty which they portrayed at the early days of marriage across the span of their relationship and they will undoubtedly reap great dividends.

A spouse who only gets interested with sex and ignores the three aspects mentioned in this pillar will end up hurting a loved spouse through selfishness. I have met many spouses complaining because their loved ones have denied them their conjugal rights. A little analysis of proceedings mostly reveals two things (1) unresolved issues that are causing dissatisfaction in the said spouse (2) A spouse's failure to consider the interest of the other one. The word of God gives a very elaborate advice on this behaviour when Paul told the Corinthian church, "Do not deprive each other except by mutual consent and for a time, so that you may devote yourselves to prayer. Then come together again so that Satan will not tempt you because of your lack of self control". 1Cor 7; 5

Spouses who are after a successful marriage will need to know how to fun up their sexual life. It is too important to be ignored. They should know very well that sex does not start in the bedroom, rather it is supported by the way the relationship developed many hours before bed time. It is unrealistic expectation for a spouse to dream for love intoxication in the bed room while the wounds of intimidation, violence, and disrespect are still fresh and not bandaged in the other spouse. Spouses in pursuit of a lasting marriage should keep a friendly relationship and resolves hurting issues, a thing that will enhance their quest for intimate fellowship.

A lady whose husband only seeks satisfying a personal sexual urge without considering her sexual needs will feel frustrated, unsatisfied and unloved and the vice versa is true. Sexual union should therefore aim to minister to both spouses otherwise regular dissatisfactions from a spouse may easily jeopardise your relationship. Spouses should prepare each other and derive joy in satisfying the needs of each another. Being considerate and bearing a mutual sense of responsibility in this act reinforces the bond of sexual intimacy.

A regular feeling of dissatisfaction after sex is hazardous for a couple

I must admit that this domain is not easy to perfect and especially considering that the sexual responses of a male and a female are different. I might not feel okay to close this paragraph without specifically advising men to slow down while trending on this area. Lack of skill in this area makes many men to rush to fulfil their instant sexual desires without considering the desires of their spouses.

Passion in a wider context is a combination of attractiveness and sexual desires. If it operates in isolation it may be like lust. It touches the soul, the mind and the body. It is important for couples to equip themselves with relevant knowledge and skills on this matter to avoid hurts and disappointments.

1) Do you really love your spouse, or you used to?

2) How do you demonstrate your love to your spouse?

3) How do you make your spouse remain attracted to you?

Take time and dissect each of the above questions allowing yourself moments to pause and genuinely reflect on how successful you have been in this area and what you can do to bring a change. Love is a mystery which those in pursuit of a successful marriage must discover. Marriage without love is empty and void as it operates outside God's guideline on the same. Remember what Apostle Paul said about love in 1Corinthians 13:4-8a: Love is patient, love is kind, it does not envy, it does not boast, it is not proud. It is not rude; it is not self seeking, it is not easily angered, it keeps no record of wrongs, Love does not delight in evil but rejoices with the truth. It always protects, always trusts, always hopes, and always perseveres. Love never fails.

> *A spouse should first be a love partner and then a sexual a partner*

2) Intimacy

Love

This could be defined as close familiarity or friendship where thoughts and feelings are shared. It is entirely vital for any couple who envisage a successful marriage that they cultivate the intimacy dimension of love in their relationship. Intimacy is pivotal to continuity of a relationship. It asks questions like: "How can I know that you love me?" Delilah won Samson because she laid emphasis on this area. She wanted to live with someone who is open, and who would not die with secrets. After Samson failed to open his heart to Delilah three times, she had this to tell him, "Then she said to him, "How can you say, 'I love you', when you won't confide in me? **Judges 16:15**. Actually the scripture shows Delilah as someone who was looking for love and not for sex. This is what friendship is. A spouse must be the best friend that one has.

There are many marriages where spouses are not close to each other at all, they never disclose their feelings or share ideas. In such relationships though there may be a great sense of commitment there may also be a sizeable amount of dissatisfaction. A woman may tend to feel used when her antennae sense that her husband's heart is far away. When we discovered that it does not pay to live with a stranger in the house my wife and I worked hard to become best friends. We are close at heart and we try to connect via air waves during the day when necessity separates us. We are on a project of coming out of individualism to being accountable to each other. Sometimes we forget due to our human nature but after paying some undesirable cost we always come back to our senses. Loving spouses should never ignore being accountable to each other in their actions, time, money and spiritually.

> *Marriage is a big project which gets accomplished through minor tasks*

A successful marriage must provide spouses who are ready for each other's sorrows and joy. I have not yet seen close friends who never share their experiences, fears and worries and successes. The principle, "For richer for poorer" operates in this domain and if a spouse tends to ignore it then the other one will be hurt. A leaning shoulder, a listening ear, a compassionate heart and a tender touch make a spouse feel cared for and loved. It gives assurance and an inner strength. When I feel the going has weathered me, I seek to relax on the bosom of my closest friend in addition to my prayers because I know that if I fall she will raise me up, and if am cold she will be my warmth. Life has many cold experiences and couples can generate relevant warmth from an intimacy blanket.

a) Are you touched by what worries your spouse?

b) Is your spouse your best friend?

c) How secretive are you to your spouse?

> *Passion without intimacy produces infactuated love*

There can be sharp divisions along opinion lines to the extent of separation if couples have not strongly developed this domain of intimacy. God gave instructions for remaining united when joining Adam and Eve in marriage. Later Jesus repeated the same words and gave a further clarity when he said, "Haven't you read," He replied, "that at the beginning the creator made them male and female, and said, for this reason a man will leave his father and mother and be united to his wife, and the two will become one flesh? *So they are no longer two but one.* Therefore what God has joined together, let man not separate". Mathew 19:4-6

3) Commitment

Commitment may be described as a pledge or an undertaking (Oxford concise dictionary). It is a decision to keep the relationship alive and to remain with a spouse permanently. Marriage is a companionship between two people (a man and a woman) which is expected to develop and last for a life time.

This life-long nature dictates that the initiators cultivate responsibility or duty to their relationship so that it will survive this time span. The two must lead a life governed by the pledge of allegiance to each other and to the very institution of marriage.

Commitment to marriage is that which produces a lifelong relationship. This life should not be a strain or a pain as so many people have experienced. There are many spouses who endure their every hour of togetherness because their relationship lacks total surrender and is not self giving. A common scripture that is known by many people from their childhood teaches us about the nature of self giving love: *"For God so loved the world that He gave his only begotten son that whosoever believes in him shall not perish but shall have eternal life"*. John 3:16. He loved therefore he gave or he gave because he loved. Likewise marriage must be self giving if it has to reflect Christ and be seen as a success.

Paul advices the Ephesus church through the following admonition, *"Wives, submit to your husbands as to the Lord. For the husband is the head of the wife as Christ is the head of the Church, his body, of which he is the saviour. Now as the Church submits to Christ, so also wives should submit to their husbands in everything. Husbands, love your wives, just as Christ loved the Church and gave himself up for her to make her holy, cleansing her by the washing with water through the word, and to present her to himself as a radiant Church, without stain or wrinkle or any other blemish but holy and blameless. In the same way husbands ought to love their wives as their own bodies. He who loves his wife loves himself"* Ephesians 5: 22-28

God is the author of marriage and the wise can derive marriage principles from him. Commitment in marriage does not depend on circumstances; it is an all season condition that you ascribe to for the benefit of your marriage. My wife and I have come to appreciate that each of us has something to give for the enrichment of our marriage. Time, openness and participation in all family agendas without grumbling have proved a good yard stick for commitment in our marriage relationship.

Commitment therefore is love that gives without counting the cost. It gives love in abundance and without reservation to a spouse who actually is a soul mate, a best friend, the only sexual partner, a confidant, a helper, a provider, a covenant partner. It is love in extravagance. This is the love that will provide when there is need within marriage. We have many spouses in marriage whose resources are private and not in union within marriage. Marriage without commitment will not last.

> *Commitment is a major lifeline in a marriage realtionship*

The scripture says *"For where your treasure is, there will your heart be also"* Luke 12:34. Commitment is where a spouse has surrendered totally to the other and with all willingness is ready to build marriage together. Divorce is very scarce where this dimension of love is practised. There will never be a successful marriage without spouses being committed to each. It is important to know that this dimension alone is not enough to sustain a successful marriage. Actually commitment without intimacy and passion will only produce an empty love.

A consummated love will be described as one in which passion, intimacy and commitment works. Any other combination of these three will produce a relationship which is not very supportive to a lasting successful marriage.

> *While divorce scatters apart commitment gathers together*

a) How committed are you in your marriage?

b) Does your commitment depend on circumstances?

Take time and dissect each of the questions in all the three dimensions of love described in this pillar. Allow yourselves *pause moments* to creatively think how successful you have been in this area and what you can do to bring a change. Love is not dispensable in marriage; it is pivotal in marriage, the very backbone that holds or supports t he marriage structure. In a successful marriage love needs to be cultivated ferociously because it the bonding adhesive that keeps a couple together. Couples who bond without love grow weary and disinterested with each other within time. Their relationship is not only dry but also unconventional in all its functionality.

CHAPTER 2

Pillar two

Vision

"Where there is no Vision people casts restraint" Proverbs 19:28,

This pillar of vision is about foresight or good judgment in planning. Vision is the ability to see things. In optical language we learn of two types of sights namely short and long. One sees things that are near and the other sees things that are far off. A marriage vision must have both sights, that is, it needs to be a bi-focal vision. It is a summation of all the dreams, aspirations, and prayers. The husband being the head of the family should be able to produce a blue print for his marriage vision. The vision that he has is what will determine the direction that his marriage will follow. The vision should be shared with the wife right from the start.

Marriage vision determines speed and direction

A wife comes into a marriage loaded with ambitions and dreams in life, a thing which is expected within the life of a progressive person. It would be saddening if a woman has no dreams or aspirations in life. She enters into a marriage with anticipation and readiness to assist the man. It would do you good to remember the origin of a woman: God said, *"It is not good for a man to be alone"*. Genesis 2:18. In marriage therefore she becomes part and parcel of the man and hence the need for her to know the direction that the marriage is expected to be moving.

Marriage needs a common Vision

Before any marriage takes place it is good for the prospective couple to ask each other these important questions: what is your vision? What is your dream? An open discussion should be able to put the dreams together, filter them, drop the residue and develop the filtrate. Many marriages fail at this point when a man does not know how to unload a forward moving woman.

A visionary man needs to adopt and adapt his wife's vision into the marriage vision. A man who ignores this is likely to feel threatened by his wife when she sets her ideas into action. God gives a wife to the man and expects him to benefit from her mission. It is only an ignorant man who will not improve in performance and radiance after he has been united with a wife. A woman whose vision is ignored or ambitions not embraced by the husband might operate independently and in a different direction. If it happens, it automatically increases conflict within the relationship. I believe that a wise man should be able to destroy any environment which would add conflict into his marriage relationship.

> *A troubled marriage is a delight to no one not even a fool*

Woman in the vision

A man who understands the abilities in his woman works hard to tap them and use them for their marriage progression. I would say that life without active participation of a woman will certainly come to a halt. A woman has special qualities which any sensible and visionary man cannot afford to ignore. Take for example how she carries a pregnancy for nine months, painfully gives birth to a baby, nurtures the young with kindness, and meets her man's expectation. She is a unique creation! Just look at the role of women within the community, they have more group projects than men by far. Men who have value their wives understand that involving their wives in their marriage vision as equal participants rather than confused spectators tantamount to motorising their vision. It will bear more fruit and without much a delay.

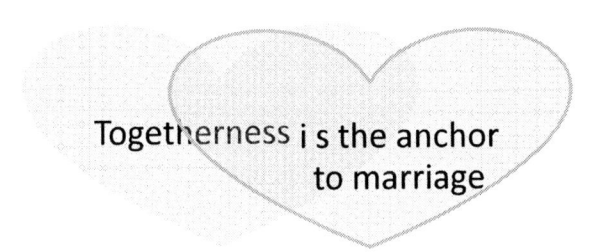

Togetherness is the anchor to marriage

The challenge would only be if the man has no vision for his marriage. I thank God that we had a good time to discuss what was in our hearts right as we were courting. We embraced and adapted each other's vision and our marriage focus was launched from the same platform. We always revisit our marriage vision as life keeps changing. In a successful marriage the spouses put their strengths together and pull in one direction. Frequent updates on the vision help to keep marriage on focus.

Vision

Vision keeps marriage on track

The wife who understands the vision of her husband is able to apply her abilities on the wagon and push it in the same direction as the husband. All her career or skills become useful tools or a strong pillar in the marriage. When a marriage does not have a vision it can be swayed in any direction by other forces at anytime. Having a vision restrains a couple not to fret when they see others slide through in a different direction. It is a fact of life that we cannot be all the same and in the same direction. A family can easily come under pressure if they leave the pursuit of their vision and begin competing with other people's visions.

What a disaster if a couple never planned for the number of children that they would like to have but down the line they bring another one or two on parents' requests or friends' influence. It is important for a couple to identify the principles that they will follow diligently without wavering or being influenced because each marriage is unique. There is a lot that couples can learn from the success of others but it's undeniable fact that a successful marriage is never a photocopy of another.

1) Have you ever discussed your marriage vision?

2) Do you evaluate the marriage vision regularly?

Take time and dissect each of the above questions allowing yourself moments of pause to creatively think how successful you have been in this area and what you can do to bring a change. People without a vision lack direction and fall at whatever comes their way. They may be easily influenced by their peers and live a dissatisfied and boring lifestyle. A successful marriage will have a guiding vision engraved in the hearts of both spouses; they read it, live it and reap it.

CHAPTER 3

Pillar three

Prayer

"Again, I tell you that if two of you on earth agree about anything you ask for, it will be done for you by my father in heaven. For where two or three are gathered together in my name, there am I with them". Mat 18:19 - 20.

Prayer is the most accurate and swiftest weapon that marriage can use in their warfare. We are always engaged in spiritual warfare whose hangovers are physically manifested at times. Prayer is basically involving the God of heaven in the battles that you face upon the surface of the earth. In order to experience success in marriage a couple must embrace the vitality of prayer. The understanding that God is near and willing to help you prepares your ground for prayers. In this book we will learn about three types of prayers that would hold up successful living in a marriage relationship.

a) Prayer of faith

This type of prayer presupposes that God is able and willing to do it. Further still we see the author of practical Christian living, James the apostle emphatically putting it, *"But when he asks, he must believe and not doubt, because he who doubts is like a wave of the sea, blown and tossed by the wind. That man should not think he will receive anything from the Lord: he is double-minded man, indeed unstable in all he does"* James 1:6-8.

Faith is that quality in a believer that gives him assurance for better things despite any negative signals. It is that quality that defies the state of affairs but believing that God is able to bring a change in the very situation. If believers cast their minds on their surroundings, they tend to hear messages that point towards failure. The carnal mind is unable to penetrate beyond the physical; its climax results are backed with evidence and report from human assessors. Faith defies human evidence through creating a solution which otherwise would not have surfaced. It goes beyond what eyes can see or minds can think and fathom.

Faith defies every human evidence

Actually faith works even when things have reached a terminal stage. It speaks as if the deal is already sorted and denies anxiety a chance to torment one self. Faith makes one to change the language from negative to positive expression. I will never forget what our high school Christian union patron once told us about faith; "faith is acting like so, even when it does not seem to be so, in order for it to be so because it is supposed to be so". Faith speaks of the greatness of God while fear speaks of the greatness of a problem. Faith is having the persuasion that it will happen. This God oriented persuasion gives confidence to you as you pray over disturbing issues.

Faith in God gives peace in times of turbulence!

There have been times since we got married when the physical evidence showed defeat, failure and impossibility in our lives. In such moments we agreed to pray acknowledging that God is able to turn round the circumstances. Some few examples of moments when the signals have been red for long and very slow to change to amber and green are: when we were planning to get married and money was scarce, when we wanted a baby and it took us four year after marriage to nurse a lively boy, when we wanted to go to the United Kingdom and we were denied visa twice, When my wife wanted a scholarship for her PhD and her many applications were declined, when we were launching into the television ministry and we did not know how. In all these and many others we prayed in faith and believed that God was able to make a way. He did it! This has given us assurance that light will shine for us along the way since marriage is not *a day only* relationship.

Apostle Paul puts it clearly that, *"now unto him that is able to do exceeding abundantly above all that we ask according to the power that is at work in us".* *(Ephesians 3:20)* In a successful marriage you pray believing God for your spouse, children, business and other things that have the capacity to sabotage your success. Prayer of faith helps you to see and trust the hand of God even when the threat of your enemy appears real.

> *Faith formats you to see victory rather than defeat*

Prayer of faith sees the battalion that is on your side and builds up one's confidence that all will be well. You believe that he that is with you is greater than he that is against you. If you fail to format yourself in this position then your prayer will be of little consequence, for without faith it is impossible to please God. Prayer of faith changes marriage perspectives and allows spouses to see possibilities. A couple embraces positive change, and confess hope rather than doom when a prayer of faith is at work.

Probably the words of Apostle James would help clarify the importance of prayer of faith, *"Is any of you in trouble? He should pray, is anyone happy? Let him sing songs of praise. Is any one of you sick? He should call the elders of the church to pray over him and anoint him with oil in the name of the Lord. And the prayer offered in faith will make the sick person well: the lord will raise him up; if he has sinned he will be forgiven. Therefore confess your sins to each other and pray for each other so that you may be healed. The prayer of a righteous man is powerful and effective.* James 5: 13-16

> *Prayer of faith is major tool for a successful marriage*

b) Prayer of Consistency and persistence

Consistency in prayer comes in by developing a trend of regularity, becoming reliable or gaining steadiness in prayer discipline. People who are inconsistent pray unevenly allowing breaks of prayerlessness. Such a people who go for holiday on prayer will fail to make their prayers effective and this might hang down the marriage rafters. They are like a student who looses touch with the syllabus when he keeps missing his lessons. He may not expect the best grade even if he attends a super academy.

Consistent prayer is not an event, it is something that is periodically done and this requires determination. It goes past the Morning Prayer or the Sunday worship service. There are many Christians who desire to enjoy stable marriage yet their marriage is only backed by corporate prayers on Sunday during church worship. These are insufficient irrespective of who

Prayer

leads the prayers. Spouses need to develop personal time frame to present their requests to God, failure to which their defence is weakened. Marriage has many enemies fighting fiercely and consistent prayer attack is necessary if the enemy is to disarm. Apostle Paul told the Thessalonians' church, *"Pray continually; give thanks in all circumstances, for this is God's will for you in Christ Jesus"*. 1Thessalonian 5:17

Consistency requires discipline and drive

Persistence is a character that makes one not to give up on a matter until it is established. It is that quality in prayer that refuses to be discouraged when one fails to get the solution at the first request. It is setting of one's attitude on destiny and pushing through the rugged path to the end. The path may have discouraging features but one chooses to ignore them because of the propelling determination. Persistence in prayer can best be explained by the acronym P.U.S.H which reads as "pray until something happens". I saw this acronym on a wall hanging in my friends' house a couple of years past and it has always been a voice in my life.

Persistence never mates with defeat

Take for example a farmer who put seeds in a well prepared ground. He expects to see germination after some days. Sometimes pests (like squirrels) can unearth the seeds the same day they are planted. A wild rabbit can eat the shoots a day or two after germination. A determined farmer comes back again with seeds and replants again defying the wits of the squirrel. He also erects a scare crow to keep these enemies at the periphery of his garden. Likewise in marriage there are many pests that surface regularly when a couple sets to pray for their marriage. A couple should therefore engage in serious combat against the enemy with determination until success safely germinates and grows in their relationship.

There are many things that could stir up discouragement in a praying spouse who lacks consistence and persistence, for example if a spouse has a resident and unacceptable behaviour. Sometimes this tempts one to give up praying and leave things to chances. When a believer has developed this persistent trait in prayer then discouragement becomes an enemy not a friend. Persistent prayer paves way for change into a successful marriage. It waits with anticipation until the desired results are obtained. Couples who persevere in prayer being consistent and wearing a persistent cloak deny the devil any chance to celebrate victory over their marriage.

> *Successful people go past the barrier of discouragement*

c) Prayer of unity

Prayer of unity forms a strong chord or strand that keeps the enemy struggling. It is good to give the enemy a hard time. If you give him an easy task he will do it faster only to come back and play with you. It is good for couples to be aware of the privilege they have to deny the devil easy access to their home through prayer of agreement.

Most of the times the enemy causes disunity between spouses, a thing that blocks prayer break through, and opens a window for him. I have found it haunting when I go to pray and we are in disagreement with my wife. Apostle Peter spoke words to this effect which are of profound importance and which every man needs to know and always remember. "Husbands, in the same way be considerate as you live with your wives, and treat them with respect as weaker partner and as heirs with you of the gracious gift of life, so that nothing will hinder your prayers."1Peter 3:7

> *Prayer of unity denies the devil access into your marriage*

Our Lord and saviour Jesus Christ taught on this brand when he said *"Again, I tell you that if two of you on earth agree about anything you ask for, it will be done for you by my father in heaven. For where two or three are gathered together in my name, there am I with them"* *(Mat 18:19 -20).* This scripture can be traded well by a couple. A couple should work hard to pray in agreement. The unity of a couple whose hearts are pursuing a common goal while standing on the same faith platform can never be broken no matter the external pressure. A group of friends can also pray in unity and this is also true for a church. Agreement allows people to see the problem from the same vantage point and this eliminates obvious splits along personal interests or opinions.

Agreement allows spouses to see a problem from the same vantage point.

Successful family projects are those undertaken with blessings from both spouses. It is easier to initiate and back a project by prayer if there is agreement between a husband and the wife or between any two business partners. Prophet Amos bringing important message from the Lord asked the children of Israel whom God had identified as his own, *"Do two walk together unless they have agreed to do so.?"* Amos 3:3.

We learn more on unity based success from the construction of the tower of Babel. We are told that the descendants of Noah after the floods were determined to protect themselves from getting scattered abroad. They were of the same language, mind and purpose when they decided to build a city and a tower. The tower ascended upwards until heaven responded and confused their language. The secret of this success was their unity. A couple which will pray in unity will overcome any hurdle that hinders success.

Spouses whose tower has stagnated should seek for solution no further than in their unity department. (Genesis 11:1-5). I must admit that this is not one of the easiest things to do. There are stubborn demons that whisper lies in order to weaken the prayer of agreement. Marriage was designed to be a life of oneness and fellowship. The rate at which families have tumbled clearly shows that many couples have not developed this kind of fellowship and intimate relationship. It is my prayer that couples would know that praying in agreement is a great land mark in successful marriage.

Unity in prayer honours no limitations

Prayer of accord brings in a consolidation of faith and eliminates selfish agenda from spouses. There are fewer struggles in supporting an issue that one has prayed for in marriage. This is something that my wife and I have discovered and it has minimized arguments and discontentment. The area of prayer has been one of the deserted areas especially within marriage yet it is the most fertile ground. The enemy fights unity ferociously for he is well informed of the destruction that prayer of unity renders to his schemes.

Prayer

Prayer of unity requires a couple to be in dialogue before and after.

The greatest battle of disagreement is in the mind and it hinders the action by the heart. These disagreements in marriage can emanate from communication breakdown, financial issues, a character issue, or a spiritual disobedience. This creates a wall of separation between the hearts and unity's continuity is endangered. I believe that prayer of agreement requires open hearts. This may lead to holding of hands in prayer though holding of hands does not necessarily mean unity.

May I call the spouses to start praying together with open hearts and defying all odds to hold hands together as a sign of unity. The enemy is never happy when this method of prayer is applied for it scatters him and nullifies his intentions. With all your trying as a couple, try joint prayers which is enveloped with agreement, and you will discover the truth of the scripture which says that, "*two are better than one and the chords of three strands is not easily broken*". *(Ecclesiastes 4:9-12).* Do not wreck the success of your marriage by being indifferent as a couple. Frequent togetherness in prayer is one of the ingredients of successful prayer, a quality worth of cultivating in marriage.

1) Where have you placed prayer in your marriage?

2) How united are you as a couple in your prayers?

3) How frequently do you pray together?

Take time and dissect each of the above questions allowing yourself *pause moments* to creatively think how successful you have been in this area and what you can do to bring a change. Prayer is not dispensable; it is core in marriage the very life line that many have ignored. In a successful marriage prayer is not the last resort when all other options have failed rather it is the genesis of any sensible undertakings.

CHAPTER 4

Pillar four

Communication

Good communication network is one of the yard sticks for a developed nation. It facilitates easy and fast movement of people and goods. As nations rise up the ladder of success, a nation with good communication never lags behind. I know of certain regions in my country blessed with good climatic conditions and have enormous potential to produce dairy and horticultural products which could get into international market. Unfortunately due to poor road networks these products fail to get to the urban cities when fresh. For example some roads are impassable during rainy seasons and this hinders the marketing of the horticultural products which grow all the year round. Other areas have no railway or airport facilities. In the same way that businesses cannot succeed in an environment with poor communication so it is with marriage.

Communication allows resources to connect.

Communication in marriage involves more than talking. It is the way the mind is framed, the way we express our emotional frustrations and our joys. It is the path through which messages pass from one spouse to the other. Our marriage had very seasonal roads (muddy) in the first year, a thing that caused moments of loneliness, tears and bewilderment. When we discovered how harmful it was to move marriage on such roads we quickly shifted to an all weather road (tarmac). I would gladly say that for the last couple of years God has helped us a lot on the way we communicate with each other. We have not yet made it as communication requires daily determination due to new challenges that come along the way but we are determined to.

> *Broken communication may mean broken success*

In many of our couple counselling meetings women complain about their husbands being 'silent' family members. This is where a man opts to be silent for fear of being challenged on certain aspects in their relationship package. Other men chose to wear threatening faces and only talk sparingly when asked a question. Couples need to know that the above types of behaviour communicate through sending the unwanted signals. Therefore we can confidently say that silence speaks. A man who ignorantly uses this form of communication fails to effectively connect with the wife and may inflict pain and dissatisfaction in a relationship. In such a case their marriage moves from the success path to the failure bound one.

Bridge analogy

Communication is like a bridge across a big river and without which one can drown if attempts to cross are made. In places where geographic conditions favour great rivers to meander around its landscape, those who live on one side can only be connected to the other side via a bridge.

Communication

> As a bridge is to a big river so is communication to marriage

Goods from one side of the river are easily supplied across a bridge. The bridge also must have good structures otherwise it may fail depending on the weight above it. Spouses are like the two ridges which are separated by a great gully. They likewise must communicate effectively to allow mutual connection between them.

This sharing between a couple keeps each spouse well informed of the other's intentions, progress, challenges, fears and successes. Without good communication a spouse will try to interpret the moves, gestures or behaviours of the other one. This might lead to inaccurate or premature conclusion, suspicions, hate and anger, things which never support a successful marriage.

A successful marriage is never measured by the size of the bank account but the quality of the relationship between the couple. The quality of a relationship is dependent on understanding, openness, respect, truthfulness, unity, and trust. Good communication is therefore the nest in which this quality is hatched. One of the main segments of communication is through talk. It is a very important form of communication which couples must learn and develop if they are to enjoy a good relationship.

> *A word fitly spoken is like apples of gold in Pictures of silver (Proverbs 25:11)*

Levels of talk

Spoken communication ranges from simple talk which every human engages the other to serious intimate talk. Let me highlight four different types of talks necessary in a successful marriage.

Level 1

The first one is the general talk. This is the talk that makes life manageable, it is relational and informative. Every normal human being uses it on daily basis. It could be used at home, by friends or colleagues at the market place. Even people who do not know each other can engage in this type. It is here where spouses greet each other, talk about events on the way to work, and how the day was.

Having worked as a teacher for many years, my wife always asked me when we got home, "how were the youngsters today?" Her question allowed me to pour out any chocking difficult that probably had followed me from school. It gave me a time to empty my day's experiences and created room for a new experience with my family. I have also taken time to encourage her depending on her day's experience. This simple talk allows people to connect and couples need it as well. A successful marriage will be developed upon such a platter where a spouse's connectivity is embraced and encouraged.

Break the yoke of marital failure through effective communication

Level 2

The second type of communication has spices in form of jokes and gestures. This breaks the monotony and brings in laughter and sense of humour that relaxes the atmosphere. Mostly, it is used by people who know each other or new people who want to break the rigidity in a group or in a person. The

Communication

word of God tells us that, *"a cheerful heart is good medicine"* Proverbs 17:22. The appetizer for an effective communication in a marriage is squeezed out of the informal talks, where jokes, stories, and casual talk are entertained.

Laughter brings issues of healing.

It is good for couples to develop this type of talk to the highest level. A couple can even create their own code of talk which will bring fun in their talk thus denying stress an opportunity. This gives some uniqueness in the marriage and gives a sense of connectivity whenever it's used. In our marriage we enjoy this type of informal talk very frequently; we have created our jargon that nobody else would know what we mean. They bring laughter whenever we use them. Marriage should not be a stale piece of bread that you struggle to eat; rather there should be plenty of fun.

It is not fitting for a spouse to fail to cause laughter at home but be the chief entertainer elsewhere. It is good for spouses to start at home and then the overflow get to others. Those who aspire for a successful marriage will ensure that their spouses enjoy all their jokes, watch all their gymnastics, and listen to all their tales. Your spouse and children need to hear your stories at home not at the gallery.

This type of communication allows children to connect with their dads or mums with ease. The environment relaxes and parents can use it to efficiently pass vital information to their children informally. Couples should therefore use this as a tool to enrich their marriage. It is stress free and not repelled even by teenagers. In this level even visitors can enjoy the progress and make their input also. It is a mixed grill type of communication.

Level 3

The third level of communication is where serious matters are discussed. This time a couple is seeking to address some issues that need attention. In this level one brings in personal opinions and suggestions fitting to their marriage dream or vision. A spouse has freedom to contribute and his/her ideas should be brought on board into the marriage cart.

Somebody could hear of this and say, no way! My culture does not allow women to talk! Some of these cultural practices have their time lapse gone and need an informed replacement. People often fear to break from what they are used to even if it brings no benefit to them and that is slavery of mind. It has been said that successful people are those who are willing to do what the unsuccessful people fail to do. Remember marriage is a union of two members who are equal in value and only different in traits. Those who fail to understand this tends to incline importance towards one personality, and in most culture towards the male side. We are in a dispensation where revelation from the word of God has brought us liberation from the cultural bondage which for ages has undermined the contribution of a female spouse at home. It is true that spouses who give their opinions feel honoured and add diversity and balance to their marriage which are good toll stations for a successful marriage.

This level of communication may be at the level of a family business meeting where spouses listen, pause, question and contribute their ideas. One spouse might share an idea and then ask the opinion of the other one. I cannot count the times that my wife and I have asked for each other's opinion on delicate and simple matters too. There is a time to listen to each other's contribution and to bear with the criticism that will follow. I would call it a shearing time. A sheep keeps its cool when the shearer is cutting the wool but afterwards it looks cleaner.

It is at this level where decisions that endorse a move or a change in their marriage are made by a couple. In a successful marriage therefore each spouse is involved in major decision making. I would hate to remember how in our culture women were ignored and made to be of no influence. They were never involved in decision making. Men decided everything! No wonder there were no accelerated developments. That dispensation is gone and now men who desire to cultivate lasting relationships must include their wives in decision making.

I must confess that I enjoy having a forward thinking wife whose ideas and criticism I kindly embrace. This does not make things easy for an egocentric minded man. It requires a man to exercise maturity and understanding of the role that his wife came to fulfil. I enjoy listening to her opinion or school of thought in certain matters before making a decision. In decision making it is important that your idea be fully challenged by your spouse until both of you node for its viability. This is not always sweet but it is the healthiest check point before embracing it as a marriage or family project.

Analyse an issue before making a decision.

Do you jointly discuss serious matter that affects your marriage?

Level 4

The fourth level of communication is where a spouse expresses feelings and emotions. A spouse could be feeling some level of dissatisfaction emanating from a range of sources such as dysfunctional sex life, financial wastage, work based anxiety, fears of an anticipated failure, or a spouse's disturbing behaviour.

This level of dialogue is very delicate and it makes men to shake if they know that their wives are calling them to discuss issues they would otherwise not. This is an area of make or break. It is a level where spouses cry, lament, complain, separate and divorce. It therefore cannot be treated lightly. In this level some spouses feel deep pain, walk in shame, fear infections from unfaithful spouses, experience violence and live in an uncertain environment. All these causes emotional bleeding and those in pursuit of a successful marriage must handle it with wisdom, care and urgency.

> *Emotions frequently ignored may gradually invite marital break down*

This area requires maturity, understanding and selflessness. I have found couples who blame each other vehemently and are unwilling to take responsibility of their actions; unfortunately they end up hurting each other deeply. It is important while at this level of talk that spouses be fair on each other a thing that will reduce unjustified accusation.

In a successful marriage spouses seek to heal each other. The best thing that a spouse can do to a loved one is to accept the mistake and ask for forgiveness as opposed to just saying "I am sorry". Owning up a mistake (probably saying, "I was on the wrong") is the starting point for genuine forgiveness. It is great failure and a disservice to marriage if a husband or wife will cheaply dismiss an issue that the other spouse has complained about. A good response shows that somebody cares and is considerate. It beats logic how one would claim to value marriage yet ignores the feelings of a loved spouse.

> *Failing to accept a mistake is a sign of immaturity*

This is the level where you come clean to each other. It is painful for a spouse to live unsatisfied because the other is not willing to settle down the matter. This level is like a surgery for marriage struggles. Spouse must be ready to accept their mistakes, show signs of remorse and ask for pardon. It undermines the intelligence of your spouse to assume that s/he is immune to your bad behaviour. Marriage is a covenant whose terms were given by God, and being careless about them not only offends God and also your spouse who feels it physically and emotionally. When spouses fail to apportion time for this level of talk, wounds remain open while trust and reliability are threatened.

Remember marriage is a union of two adults, a male and a female who have similar values, deserves respect and have equal right. They both are charged with a duty to subject themselves one to another. Those spouses who follow this principle show consideration of their spouses' feelings and the emotions. This lays a back bone of a successful marriage. It is important that the young and the old alike understand that the master versus slave mentality has no room in a lasting marriage relationship. In marriage no one is senior or junior to the other but two equal people who are submissive to each other.

Listening

Communication

It is important that spouses learn the art of listening because in marriage people must always talk through. One should listen more than he talks; The scripture has instructed to this *effect* "*My brothers take note of this; everyone should be quick to listen, slow to speak and slow to become angry, for man's anger does not bring about the righteous life that God desires*" (James 1:19). Listening shows that you respect your spouse, and it gives you an opportunity to understand the perspective of your spouse.

Listening hastens understanding

I grew up in a family of six, three boys and three girls. At times we would be noisy and especially after an exciting day. My mum would always try to initiate order and required us to listen to one another. She used to tell us that listening is the crux of living together. When I got married I discovered that listening to each other is essential to a harmonious living for a couple. Have you learnt to listen to your spouse? If not yet put effort for it pays dividends.

Listening is an art that each spouse must learn

In listening it is important for one to be interested with what the spouse is talking about. It's good to win the negative impression battle staged in one's mind when a spouse is talking. In listening it is good to be patient with the spouse and avoid pre- meditated answers which ignorant people inject while someone is talking. Making conclusion without proper listening and synthesising the information given by a spouse is a sign of immaturity in marriage.

Communication methods

Communication does not mean talking though talking is part of communication. People have different methods they use to communicate ranging from verbal to non-verbal. The non verbal could be visual expression, nodding one's head as a sign of conformity or agreement. The invention of Technological devices has allowed us to communicate over mobile phones, text messages, emails and the like. We need to use all of them to enrich communication in our marriage if we desire to enjoy a fruitful marriage. The ability to choose which type to use at different levels of communication is called wisdom.

> *A premature answer is a great hindrance to communication*

Hindrances to communication

In Communication, the system has three stations namely the source, the medium through which the message passes and the recipient. Taking an example of spoken communication, the source would mean the person talking: the recipient is the person listening; the medium is where the message will pass, in this case air.

In successful communication spouses must ensure that clear information leaves the source, and that it is received by the recipient with similar clarity. Communication breakdown come when there is obstruction between the source and the recipient.

Anything that hinders clarity and easy flow of message from the source to the recipient may be considered as noise. Consider the following scenarios and their effect to good communication:

i. Talking to your spouse while facing a different direction
ii. Talking to your spouse while in a different room
iii. Talking to your spouse as you walk away
iv. Watching a favourite program on the television while engaged in a serious talk with your spouse
v. Unfavourable body condition e.g. illness and tiredness.

All these conditions will affect communication in one way or another. Those with a desire for a successful marriage will seek to be effective in their communication by seizing the right environment.

> *A premature conclsion is a sign of immaturity. Be quick to hear and slow to speak.*

Another hindrance to communication in marriage is having wrong attitude or pride. This kind of inclination hinders one's understanding and perception. A spouse who harbours pride and arrogance blocks any contribution from the other one. This mind set produces a holier than thou attitude which consequently undermines the spouse's contribution. An undermined spouse lives at the periphery with a reserved view. If this condition remains for long it could also lead to low self esteem and kill the creativity and enthusiasm that is necessary in a successful marriage.

> *Pride and arrogance are never siblings of a good marriage*

One of the things that have improved communication in our marriage is the ability to listen without being judgemental even the temptation is biting. We had to make a resolve of holding any comment until the other has finished self expression. We are still working on this project but at least we value each other's contribution even when we don't agree. It is good to appreciate that there will be differences in opinions, understanding, and velocity in any communication. If your spouse is fast then pave a way and never try to limit him/her by putting blocks. If he/she is slow, check if there is clarity in your communication.

1) What is your attitude on your spouse's contribution?

2) Is there dialogue in your marriage or do you dictate?

3) What is the greatest hindrance for good communication in your family?

Take time and dissect each of the above questions allowing yourself *pause moments* to honestly think how successful you have been in this area and what you can do to bring a change. Good communication works for all including babes, but the absence of it may hurt the wise and even a king. Therefore work hard and effectively communicate with your spouse if at all your marriage is to be a success. Remember that your marriage is not a rehearsal; therefore make good use of your opportunity.

> *Marriage is a union between two adults, a male and a female bearing the same values though possessing different traits*

CHAPTER 5

Pillar five

Finances

Solomon the wise and rich king made a profound statement which all families seeking to be successful need to adapt. The statement is;

> "*Money answers all things*" *Ecclesiastes 10:19*

What a profound statement that families can embrace from King Solomon who was both rich and wise. Money is the medium of exchange of everything that we have apart from life and the gifting that are endued by God. It is a force that has the ability to do constructive and destructive work depending on who has it. Many couples who have put their money in a constructive expenditure tends to live a luxurious life while the others have been deeply hurt to a point of mental break down and even divorce through its destructive force. Finances or wealth is therefore an area in marriages that need to be thoughtfully handled, given priority and supported by prayer.

In this pillar we will look at the making of money, expending it, and being financially accountable in marriage.

a) Making money

It is important that a marriage has definite avenues of acquiring money, probably wealth for those whose eyes are open. These could be either business or employment in a broader sense. The starting point is never the same for all families. Some people rely on a career pursuit; others have a lot of inheritance to develop, while others seize wealth creation opportunities that life and creativity brings.

The cost of living has been on the rise and sometimes sharply based on global economic stability. A family with a single income is likely to struggle and tremble beyond measure especially if one is on low income band. It is expedient for a family to have multiple avenues to increase their earning power. Couples should put their efforts together and use their skills and creativity to generate wealth. In the modern days we cannot underrate the potential that women have in wealth creation. Nowadays they are more educated than men, the barriers have been broken and there is no longer any ceiling hindering their upward mobility in careers.

Women who value their families will never allow pride to overtake them thus undermining their husbands when their earning power over do that of their husbands. This is an issue that has brought friction and actually destruction in marriages. A couple need to establish the financial frame work for their family which recognises all the earnings as family money. This dispels pride or arrogance that the earning spouse might project to the other. When such a frame work is in place it massages the male ego which never accepts being overtaken by a woman. The degree of earning does not guarantee superiority in a marriage union where love and openness are practiced. It is only the immature spouses and those who have missed the spirit of togetherness who will display pride or attitude to each other because of ones' higher earnings position.

> *Riches without wisdom is a deadly trap*

It would be great for an individual or a couple to be equipped with skills that would add their earning value to them. These skills will place you on a demand list and make you step on the upper rungs of a success ladder. Coupled with skills, abilities and creativity it is good to ask for God's favour for it is him who opens doors which no man can shut. The scripture says *"behold it is God who gives you power to make wealth".* (Deuteronomy 8:18)

It is good for a family to pray for divine ideas which they can develop using their skills and creativity to become sources of income. Whatever ideas that you get think big about it and work on it with all dynamism. Ensure that your idea is developed to high quality and operate with integrity to avoid back firing. Once you get an idea move fast being careful not to entertain launching phobia, a thing which makes people to go circles.

b) Financial needs

The reason for making money or getting wealth is to meet with the needs (current and future) of a marriage set up. They may range from daily expenditure for food, shelter, leisure to other planned investments. Education is another major area which could be treated as an investment both for the spouses and their offspring. I would strongly recommend that each couple budget for personal development. Old skills are getting outdated fast, and there are enough challenges to exhaust the old energy. There is need for renewal through formal training, being coached or mentored. The best mentor or coach should be one you emulate whose character is despicable and has your interest at heart.

This era needs spouses who are informed not only in making money but also in prioritised expenditure. A marriage that has good leadership enjoys good planning which yields to appropriate prioritising.

HOW MUCH DOES HE EARN? HOW MUCH DOES OUR FAMILY HAS?

MY EARNINGS IS MY SECRET? HIS EARNING SHOULD NOT BE SECRET!!!!!

c) Accountability

During our period of dealing with marriage ministry we have met families whose main challenge is lack of accountability in the area of finances. Accountability is crucial to any marriage that desires to be successful. It eliminates suspicion and sheds light in the area of conflict and doubt. Money like any consumable supplies can easily vanish depending on the usage. My dad (Peter) used to tell us, "There is no little money if it's well planned and there is no much money where extravagance reigns". It never meant much then but today I treasure every letter in his phrase. Thanks million times oh my dad.

> *Accountability breaks the yoke of suspicion*

A good point to start is for spouses to be open to each other on their earnings. It is quite a surprise the number of spouses that I have interacted with who want to enjoy a good marriage yet operate in private rooms when it comes to finances. It is disturbing how people sleep in one bed, under the same blanket and intimately get to know each other yet fail to be open on their finances.

Jesus gave a statement, *"For where your treasure is, there will your heart be also"* (Luke 12:34). It is therefore advisable for a loving man to invest in his wife and vice versa. This would draw their hearts together and closer to each other. Spouses whose hearts are wrapped together in a common goal never do things out of selfishness. They spend their energy and time on those things which are within their marriage goal. I thank God that my wife knows about all our finances as well as I do. She has access to all the accounts and statements. This is what we call *open-open policy* and it works very well for people who love, and trust each other. It is imperative to understand that marriage will never be a success if accountability is treated as anathema.

> *Successful marriage is where spouses open and close their wallets together*

There are many spouses who daily hurt each other through expenditure that tantamount to extravagance and lack of wisdom. Take an example of a spouse who replaces the family car with brand new Ferrari sports car, while their rent, household bills and their daughter's nursery fee are not paid. This may increase the marriage pulse rate and introduce a crack within the trust fabric. As a matter of principle it is good for family expenditure to be in line with family budget. It is less painful to follow budget where spouses are open to each other than the agony and suspicion that extravagance or lack of accountability causes in marriage.

> *Openness denies suspicion a foothold*

In the course of time during our marriage there has been many times that our needs have exceeded our earnings, a thing that automatically introduces strains. At such moments of low key we have sought to be patient with each other, have together prayed and sought for a way out.

> *If you are not together at the bottom do not expect to climb up together*

1) Are you open to your spouse on your finances?

2) Have you utilised all relevant skills to make wealth?

3) Is your wealth more than your needs?

Take time and dissect each of the above questions allowing yourself *pause moments* to honestly think how successful you have been in this area and what you can do to bring a change. The state of affluence does not guarantee successful marriage but a successful marriage has financial wellbeing as a yard stick.

CHAPTER 6

Pillar six

Character

Character is defined as distinguishing qualities or temperaments. It is that which sustains one's moral fibre. Other words that could define character are distinctiveness, attributes, individuality and manner. The scripture reveals the importance of good character *"A good name is better than fine perfume"* Ecclesiastes 7:1a. It is better to have a good name than being popular. A person may be famous but have a negative image. When we were growing up in our village families were defined on the line of character, there were those that we were warned of and there were those we were challenged to emulate.

Character is one of those inner attributes that drive one into actions which are rated either as acceptable or unacceptable standard. It is good to note that the standard or the measuring rod of a good character is the infallible word of God. If this standard is ignored, the consequences are grave as the marriage start a gradual tremor or decay. This affects all the other pillars we have highlighted as important. Character is not a commodity bought off the counter rather it is a quality that is developed through serious discipline and obedience to the word of God.

In a successful marriage character is more valued than fame.

All of us at one point in life are faced with undesired practices that knock at our doors wanting to master some areas of our lives. This could be a strong influence from a friend, a trend of disobeying God's word, pride of achievement, unwholesome talk, or strange relationship just to mention a few. Marriage would not be successful if it is grabbed and controlled by these practices. It should be a personal responsibility to battle any negative trend working against one's marriage. This kind of battle will only be worn by applying the inerrant word of God for it has power to destroy any satanic impulse.

Apostle Paul made it clear in the following scripture, "The *weapons we fight with are not the weapons of the world. On the contrary, they have divine power to demolish strongholds. We demolish arguments and every pretension that sets up against the knowledge of God, and we take captive every thought to make it obedient to Christ. This resolve will best be enhanced by the knowledge of the word of God.*" 2Corinthians 10; 4-6

It is a vain thing to build marriage upon men's philosophy or tradition because they lack reliability. Men are prone to weakness and their theories or principles can easily mislead if they are not biblically based. We do not have to go far to know the limitations of man, we just need to open our eyes and the trend of man's behaviour is as clear as sky. Jesus, the great teacher, taught, "*Ye shall know them by their fruits. Do men gather grapes of thorns or figs of thistles? Likewise every good tree bears good fruit; but a corrupt (bad) tree bears bad fruits. Every tree that does not bear good fruit is cut down and thrown into the fire. Thus by their fruit you will recognize them".* Mathew 7:16-20.

It should be a personal challenge for one to pursue those qualities that will not be sour when tasted by one's spouse. These tasty qualities are the ones that define a good character and vice versa. Character like salvation is a full time practise that a couple should strive to achieve. I have met spouses complaining of strange discoveries about their spouses. Such discoveries always disturb the equilibrium of a loving spouse whose trust is left betrayed. Couples who consistently work towards attaining character within the frame work of God's word create an environment conducive to nurture aspects of a successful marriage.

Technology and character

We all have opportunity in this era of technology to access the whole world without moving away from our regions. The internet is a very useful tool yet surrounded by many fierce predators seeking for a culprit. Adult Chat rooms have facilitated spouses to be engaged in unhealthy dating, a thing which negates a spouse's commitment to marriage. Pornographic surfing is also a vice on the rise and has shattered marriages of both the lay men and the clergy. Text messages or just a call from a mobile can also be a down turn for one's character. Seeing that this is the dispensation in which we are living what kind of spouses ought we to be?

A prudent man sees danger and takes refuge, but the simple keep going and suffer for it. Proverbs 22:3

It is very hard to police one's spouse for technology will log you out, but being responsible as a person and keeping clear conscience is the best police man. It is important to mention that character is not necessarily what is seen (technology has brought a delete button) but who you are from the inside.

Technological temptations need technological boundary

Seeing that to ruin a character is just a button away what manner of a spouse should one be? This is a question that individual spouses need to address and then discuss it together as a couple if the fruits of a successful marriage are to be reaped. Seeing that technological temptations are live spouses need to build strong boundaries or high walls against the vice. Addiction comes after the senses have had an exposure to the vice more than once. If the boundaries are not respected then character will be at stake and this does not spare the standing of a marriage. Couples who frequently edify themselves with the word of God will understand that some sites, or programs are designed by men of reprobate minds, and will therefore refrain themselves from casting a glance on such vanity.

Apostle Paul while on trial before Felix said words of profound nature in shaping our character, *"So I strive always to keep my conscience clear before God and man."* Acts 24:16. I recommend that you use this truth to reinforce your character even when your spouse is out of sight.

We frequently get complaints from women about their husbands who spend all their times at home on the computer while men complain about their wives being preoccupied with television and telephone. If spouses are not careful they can form appalling patterns on the technological gadgets which rip off their quality time with each other or with Children.

1. Do you have any fears for your marriage emanating from technology? (E.g. internet, Television or telephone)
2. Have you discussed and created some boundaries technologically?
3. Do you overdo your technology antics and then have no quality time with your spouse?

Social life and character

Others have entertained coarse jokes and seductive communication with colleagues, service providers, and former school mates. Do you know that if one opens a window for the devil it is not an angel who will go through. Think about spouses who expose themselves to unethical music, nasty programs over the television or in the cinema halls. A spouse needs to understand that whatever one allows into his/her life will never leave on its own accord. This is the very thing that will shape your character.

> *If you open a window for the devil, do not expect an angel to get in!*

Think of a spouse who engages in drinking spree, or who is not faithful in his dealings. If this does not stop it tends to develop into a practice. This practice in return tends to destroy the inner conscience which ruins one's sincerity and integrity. These things happen when a spouse does not have a hedge of protection for his/her heart. The Devil gets a foothold into one's heart when one become careless and not diligent to be trained by the word of God. When this happens it ruins the character and the quality of marriage deteriorates. It is beyond imagination to expect bad character to produce an excellent marriage unless within the context of pretence.

"Make a tree good and its fruits will be good, or make a tree bad and its fruit will be bad, for a tree is recognized by its fruit." Mathew 12:33.

Character in public life

I have seen an unimpressive thing upon the earth where a spouse behaves like a little demon at home while making a great public appeal. A charismatic or eloquent leader who lacks good character may destroy own conscience in the long run. Others think that doing fine in some few areas at home is a sufficient ticket for them to have loose practices while away from home. A spouse who behaves this way might get hot reaction from the partner when the matter is discovered. My experience in the family ministry has taught me that it does not take long for a hypocritical spouse to be discovered by the other one.

A marriage mask does not survive for all seasons

I thank God that we discovered masks give the wrong impression, and consequently emptiness that does not produce any marital contentment. As a result my wife and I have been working hard to keep off mask out of our character. This requires great effort and determination as some masks camouflage while others have wings to fly back. People like to appear good before others and therefore keeping off the mask is against human nature. Remember Adam and Eve? They ate the forbidden fruit and then covered themselves with twigs. When Adam responded to God he had the best excuse, he was innocent were it not for the wife. When it was Eve's turn, she also had a great excuse, she was innocent were it not for the serpent. Their mask did not avert the consequences of disobedience. They were removed from the land of privileges.

> *For good character, seeks to impress God rather than men*

Mask cannot fall off one's face without paying a sufficient cost. This happens when you cease from being men pleaser and you seek to please God through doing the right thing for your marriage. Successful marriage thrives in an environment where spouses focus on God, work on themselves as individuals and operate an accountability partnership.

Tongue and Character

It is quite damaging for a spouse whose marriage partner has an abusive tongue or who uses the tongue with disrespect. The tongue is a boneless tissue that coils itself after uttering words unspeakable. Thanks to God that the tongue was not made the master, it can only say what it is allowed to say by the heart. The scripture puts it like this *"The tongue is fire and a world of iniquity and can defile a body being ignited by hell"* (James 3:6). This reveals that the devil is in control of so many whose tongues produces unwholesome talk. I cannot emphasize it more that the tongue has ability to be used for a good cause. Individuals must master their flexible organ and just like a Mule is put under control. Winners control their tongues and enjoy the fruit of their lips.

Spoken word carries tonnes of destructive or constructive powers. King Solomon used no lesser words in Proverbs 18:21, *"The tongue has the power of life and death, and those who love it will eat its fruit"*. I would be right to say, "Show me a perfect man and I will show you a man who takes care of his words." In a successful marriage words are seasoned with salt and are never used as agents of death to the spouse or others.

Negative meditation will never breed Positive character

I said, "I will watch my ways and keep my tongue from sin; I will put a muzzle on my mouth as long as the wicked are in my presence."Psalms 39:1

What a joy if in your marriage you would be inclined to the prayer that the Psalmist made in Psalms 19:14, *"May the words of my mouth and the meditation of my heart be pleasing in your sight, O Lord, my Rock and my redeemer"*. Our meditation develops action which then develops to character. Negative meditation breeds negative character. It is therefore important for a spouse to have a hedge of protection round the heart for out of it character is nurtured. The scripture tells us that *"above all that you guard, guard your heart for from it comes issues of life"*. Proverbs 4:23

1) Do you wear any mask to hide the 'negative you'?

2) Do you take care of your tongue, the words that you speak?

3) Would you rate your character genuinely good for marriage?

Take time and dissect each of the above questions allowing yourself *pause moments* to honestly think how successful you have been in this area and what you can do to bring a change. Knowledge, charisma, or wealth without character opens the flood gates of ruin or destruction to the person. This means that character is like a litmus paper, it tests one's reliability and validity in a marriage context. It is for a couple's advantage to know that character failure produces betrayal and may lead to a sense of dissatisfaction in marriage. More than 50% of the women who were given divorce in the UK in 2004 cited spouse's behaviour (character) as the main reason.

CHAPTER 7

Pillar Seven

Respect

However, each one of you must love his wife as he loves himself, and the wife must respect her husband. Eph 5: 33

Respect is that quality in a person that facilitates treating the other one with considerations, thus refraining from tempting or offending that person's feelings. In marriage two people agree to live together in spite of their differences. Respect will therefore allow smooth interface between the two, and without it there will always be conflicts and disagreements. A self-centred person who cannot easily accommodate a different view will experience a rocky relationship, and be a hindrance to nurturing of a successful relationship.

Trust on the other hand is that quality that makes one to have faith in a spouse. This means that a spouse feels secure having entrusted his/her life in the hands of another person. One becomes open to this person because he/she is a covenant partner in life. When this quality is at work a spouse becomes dependent on the other one without fear or suspicion: a thing that is necessary for successful marriage.

> *Dependence and interpendence are not optional in marriage; They are values worth attaining!*

People who respect each other will never do things out of their selfish agenda; they will consider the contribution of their spouses. The Philippians church was advised by Apostle Paul in the following manner, *"Do nothing out of selfish ambition or vain conceit, but in humility consider others better than yourself. Each of you should look not only to your own interests but also to the interest of others"*. Philippians 2:3-4. Respect and Trust therefore cannot be ignored in marriage as they tend to be the window upon which joy and peace comes in. Two people who respect and trust each other are likely to fly the highest and land safely on any platform.

$$\frac{\text{To get it}}{\textbf{RESPECT}}\text{ you must give it.}$$

In general people respect what they know and identify with. There is also a big tendency to fear what you do not know. This means spouses who close up might be feared and never respected by their spouses and children. On the contrary couples who are open to each other are likely to enjoy the sweet drops that ooze from the respect fountain.

We have met spouses who spend lots of their energy and effort trying to change each other. It is good if that is possible and much so if the change is for the benefit of the marriage. In family rebuild we have a phrase which many people like when they read it, "do not seek to change your spouse for your spouse might only be compatible to a changed you" A spouse who willingly changes certain aspects of a conduct certainly commands respect from the other spouse.

There are those who think of themselves as mister or miss perfect, and therefore rule out any option of changing any aspects of their lives. They blame their spouses vehemently for everything, including their own mistakes. They never enjoy their marriage for it is blocked by their ignorance, and the bible calls them fools.

"The way of a fool seems right to him but a wise man listens to advice" **Proverbs 12:15**

Enforcing a change that has no value to add in a marriage is a mere waste of time and resource. There are some changes that open a window of respect, and there is a level of respect that activates a change in a spouse. Spouses who respect each other will not find it difficult to accept each other and vice versa. Respect and trust in a marriage acts as a catalyst which allows spouses to develop faith in each other. It follows that respect is reciprocal, a two way system. When respect is at work it opens the birth canal of good things in the marriage. Actually, spouse who respect and trust each other will find it easy to sacrifice themselves for the benefit of their marriage.

Respect activates positive change; positive change enhances respect

A relationship which makes one to feel to be the master and the other a servant will generate fear rather than respect. There are many spouses in different cultures where marriages are sustained by fear and not respect.

In such a marriage freedom is not enriched but spouses endure long years in marital bondage. Spouses in such a relationship feel intimidated and their rights denied. This may lead to a spouse loosing a sense of worth and feels used rather than loved. This kind of feeling can make a spouse to walk out of the relationship or to seek help from lobby groups or friends if not parents. Christ calls us into liberty and such a relationship is not within his divine plan for us.

A lasting marriage relationship should have Christ–Church relationship where respect is reciprocal; rights and freedom are jointly esteemed. It is of importance to consider how you talk to your spouse; is your talk sandwiched with abuses, sarcasm or kindness and good will? Cultures that taught disrespect to wives have been regenerated through the power of the Gospel to say the least. This has dethroned the cultural sponsored reign of male dictatorship in the marriage.

In that era ignorance and disrespect fuelled the constitution. Today the word of God (which is the manual for marriage) has shed light on us. The scriptures have deeply taught us about the principle of sowing and reaping which is applicable in many areas in marriage. Therefore, it is absurdity for a spouse to expect respect when he/she has sown nothing taking into account culture, race or religion. This shows that respect only germinates from a seed of respect.

Sow Respect and you will reap respect

If a man fist handily control over his marriage rigidly without giving a breathing space to his wife, he will certainly be feared and that does not accord him proportionate respect. Mostly spouses who forcefully or unjustly control their partners are likely to be those who are unable to love and trust them. I have found out that work become easier in marriage where trust is embraced and practised. Spouses need to be aware of the facts that trust is not an automatic quality in marriage; it has to be worked for. Further still if trust is broken through betrayal then more work has to be done to reinstate it back.

In a successful marriage respect and trust is the cord that binds spouses together as they address life challenges which all of us have to do.

1) Do you respect and trust your spouse?

2) Does your culture make you intimidate your spouse through fear rather than demonstrate respect?

3) Do you dictate over your spouse or do you allow dialogue?

Take time and dissect each of the above questions allowing yourself *pause moments* to honestly think how successful you have been in this area and what you can do to bring a change. It is only through respect that the diversity in marriage can be made functional. In the instances where trust is not cultivated a spouse may live under constant fear of being intimidated through suspicion. The warmth of a successful marriage is anchored up by respect and trust that couples bestow upon each other.

Fear should never replace respect in marriage

It is unfortunate that people prepare and celebrate great weddings and then fail to have enjoyable marriage thereafter. A good marriage is worked for and requires strong pillars some of which we have highlighted here. Spouses should strengthen their friendship and then pull together in the same direction as navigated by their marriage vision.

CHAPTER EIGHT

The word

Reinforcing the pillars by the Word

The word of God is the belt of truth and it is what sets a standard for our lives. It surpasses every other viewpoint or cultural doctrines which men have generated over time. People from different parts of the world have their own practice and procedures which they have adapted to suit their livelihood. They have therefore defined relationships in their terms having ignored the infallible word of God; no wonder there is a global contradiction on marriage.

The traditions of men are as limited as men themselves. People are only able to govern themselves within the constraints of their knowledge but God knows everything; He understands our future and relying on him is the most solid thing that a couple can do for their marriage. God is the author of marriage and his plan was for a man to have a female companion whom they can talk on equal terms. God created a solution to the challenge that man (male) was facing and thus it's recommended that men would study more about the role of women from the scriptures. The word vividly clarifies the circumstances that made God to say, "It is not good for a man to be alone"

The Bible is the manual for right living and those who would want to have successful marriages will reap it by following biblical principles. It is in this context that we advise couples to regularly study the scriptures to get the right instructions for marital success. The Bible besides being the source of authority for Christian living gives documentations that are relevant and applicable for each of the pillars that we have discussed in this book.

Have a look at the following,

1. *Jacob worked seven years for Laban, but the time seemed like only a few days, because he **loved** Rachel so much.* Genesis 29:20. This love that Jacob had for Rachel is a demonstration of what a husband should do! Giving oneself fully for the sake of your wife and family. Jesus did the same for the sake of the church (the bride) to the point of death.

Another example of a husband who demonstrated love for his wife is Elkanah the husband to Hannah. The scripture states that, "*Whenever Elkanah offered a sacrifice, he gave some of the meat to Peninnah and some to each of her sons and daughters.[5]But he gave Hannah even more, because he loved Hannah very much, even though the LORD had kept her from having children of her own."* **1 Samuel 1:4-5.** In this case Elkanah demonstrated impartial love which is the kind needed in the family (the Agape Love). He loved Hannah even though she was barren. He understood the role of wife not in the context of just bearing children but first as a friend and a companion. He therefore encouraged and supported her despite her tainted heart as a result of Peninnah's constant ridicule of her barrenness.

2. The scripture talks of Job, a man from whom we can deduce a marriage **vision**. The scriptures say of him, *"In the land of Uz there lived a man whose name was Job. This man was blameless and upright; he feared God and shunned evil. ² He had seven sons and three daughters, ³ and he owned seven thousand sheep, three thousand camels, five hundred yoke of oxen and five hundred donkeys, and had a large number of servants. He was the greatest man among all the people of the East".* **Job 1:1-3.** This demonstrates that Job was well focused and had a good plan for his family. A man void of vision will never rise to become great at home or in the world. Greatness does not superimpose itself on a man; it is sought for through bearing a vision and translating it into reality. Again it is recorded that Job was steady when he faced severe afflictions from the enemy. His confession shows his steadiness and focus on his vision. *"I know that my redeemer lives, and that in the end he will stand on the earth, And after my skin has been destroyed, yet in my flesh I will see God; I myself will see him with my own eyes—I, and not another. How my heart yearns within me!"* Job

19:25-27. The nasty personal circumstances that surrounded him did not remove his focus from God. His wife, out of sympathy tried to persuade him to curse God so that he would be given a death penalty. Job considered her advice as being out of focus; he rebuked her severely and declined her skewed advice. When you do not have a vision you will certainly be swayed to and from depending on the surroundings.

3. Isaac was the son of the promise, a child of old age between Abraham and Sarah. He married at the age of forty and his wife Rebecca did not have children until Isaac was sixty years old. This is what the scripture describes it, *"Isaac prayed to the LORD on behalf of his wife, because she was childless. The LORD answered his prayer, and his wife Rebekah became pregnant."* Genesis 25:21. Isaac knew that prayer can bring results even in the very difficult circumstances. He refused to play the blame games as we have witnessed some spouses doing. He embraced the fact that God was able to change or reverse every curse or difficult for even Abraham had begotten him at the age of a hundred years.

4. Eli was a priest of God during the time that Samuel was born. He unfortunately did not **communicate** well with his children. He allowed them to do vile things as they served at the altar. *For I told him that I would judge his family forever because of the sin he knew about; his sons blasphemed God, and he failed to restrain them.* 1Samuel 3:13.

Word as the belt

5. Abigail was the wife of a rich man called Nabal who was also foolish. The Bible is very clear in describing the character of both spouses, *"Now the name of the man was **Nabal**; and the name of his wife Abigail: and she was a woman of good understanding, and of a beautiful countenance: but the man was churlish and evil in his doings; and he was of the house of Caleb."* 1Samuel 25; 3. The wisdom of Abigail delivered her family from the sword of David which the greediness or foolishness of Nabal had invited. Money without wisdom is disastrous. The Bible also describes another man by the name Job who was very rich. *"He owned seven thousand sheep, three thousand camels, five hundred yoke of oxen and five hundred donkeys, and had a large number of servants."* Job 1:1-3. He refused to be proud as a result of his riches. He kept his heart leaning on God even as prosperity abound.

6. David was a man after God's heart. He once killed Uriah who was the husband of Bathsheba to hide the sexual sin that he had committed with her. A number of his children also had a character problem, one of them raped his step sister, the other overthrew David as king, and another slept with David's concubine while another killed his step brother. While Job the rich man mentioned above had a clean track of record that the scripture says of him, *"This man was blameless and upright; he feared God and shunned evil"* Job 1:1. Joseph would have had a very secretive sexual affair with Potiphar's wife because he was in the house alone with her, but he refused. Joseph had the courage and confidence that emanated

from his fear of God and which made him respond: *"My master has withheld nothing from me except you, because you are his wife. How then could I do such a wicked thing and sin against God?" And though she spoke to Joseph day after day, he refused to go to bed with her or even be with her"* Genesis 39:9

7. Sarah, the wife of Abraham respected him and gave him honour both as a servant of God and also as her husband. The scripture vividly puts it; *"Even as Sara obeyed Abraham, calling him **lord**: whose daughters ye are, as long as ye do well, and are not afraid with any amazement."* 1Peter 3:6

Conclusion

Concrete beams and pillars are reinforced with steel to make them strong, withstand shakes, tension, compression, or impact loads. Without these steel bars there may be tendency for the pillars to give in to pressure that they are always subjected to by their environment. They would be brittle lacking the necessary strength. The word of God is like these metal bars and it strengthens the marriage pillars discussed above. A successful marriage will seek to be supported by strong pillars. Digging deep into the word and seeking its relevance in the various aspects represented by each of the pillars will be like adding a fourth metal bar into it.

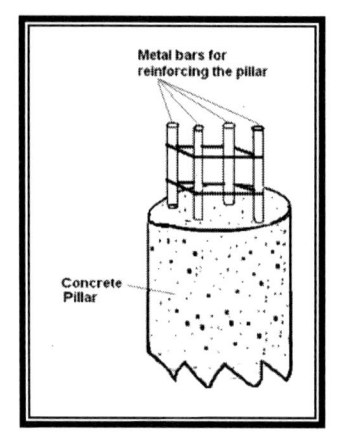

Finally, the ball is now on your court to score by first erecting each of the pillars and making it functional in your marriage. Let it be your daily ambition to strengthen the pillars that support your marriage.

If love; let it be sincere. Demonstrate it as the word has guided us.

If Vision; Let you not live without one for the sake of sustainability of your marriage and family. Let your vision be strengthened by the word.

If prayers; Strengthen it by having the right knowledge of the word. The word that you know will become your shield and your weapon of attack. Any promises that are written down can never be yours if you do not know them and prayerfully claim them.

If communication; talk to your spouse as unto a king or a queen ensuring that you are clear and respectful. Let the word teach you how to season your words that they may benefit the hearers who in this case will be your spouse and children.

If finances; Let the word teach you about love of money, prosperity and generosity. The word will reveal to you that silver and gold, cattle on a thousand hills and all the great seas belong to God. Strengthen your financial capacity through the guidance from the word.

If Character; the word has not been silent, get to know what happened to people who missed some steps on the character ladder. What about those who stepped on every rung of the ladder? How was their ending? Then learn how to strengthen yourself and bring your wife and children to read from the same script.

If respect; Learn what the scriptures teaches and you will also be respected. Respect has never been a one way valve; rather it is a give and take characteristic. The word will teach you that your spouse is your equal apart from the gender which is tailor made for its functionality. Such a person must never be treated with disrespect.

There are hidden treasures in the word and they bring riches to your relationship thus making your marriage divorce proof. Divorce is not an unbeaten monster; rather it is ignorance, foolishness and spiritual dryness that allows a man or a woman to hate a dear friend, companion and life partner whom they had earlier loved. If we be rich in the word, we will empty the granary of divorce thus disarming or making void the enemy's scheme that threatens marriage success.

Remember that there are no automatic good marriages out there; rather spouses bring in their positive input and sacrifice out of which solid foundations are laid. Spouses who fail to cooperate with each other deny their marriage valuable support and allow defeat to permeate through the marriage fibre. In such case success in their marriage will only be a mirage.

> *Success in character will never produce failure in marriage*

Please visit our website www.familyrebuild.org for more materials. All questions should be directed to familyrebuild@yahoo.co.uk.

Whatever you know will become your weapon of warfare.

Other books by Peter

- Understanding the British system of Education (ISBN 978-1-907 188 16-9), co-authored with Mr.Kamotho.
- Embracing responsible relationship and sexual purity (ISBN 978 -1-907 188 -24-4)
- Embracing change (ISBN-978-1-907-188-25-1) A very important book on personal development.

Appeal for Salvation

In case you have not known Jesus as Lord and saviour of your life, this can be a golden opportunity for you to know him. Know that Jesus loves you and he died on the cross for your sins. He desires to forgive and make you whole.
If you believe this and would like to invite him into your heart, please pray this prayer;
Lord Jesus, I am a sinner! I come to you for mercy and I do confess my sins and wickedness. I believe in my heart that you died for my sins. I invite you to be my Lord and saviour.
In case you have made this prayer, please go to a bible teaching church and introduce yourself to the pastor or any mature Christian that you know. You could also let us know and we will send you more spiritual help.